THE

BURNING

WORLD

ARROWSMITH
PRESS

Also by Sherod Santos

Poetry
Accidental Weather
The Southern Reaches
The City of Women
The Pilot Star Elegies
The Perishing
The Intricated Soul
Square Inch Hours

Essays
A Poetry of Two Minds

Translations
Greek Lyric Poetry: A New Translation

THE

BURNING

WORLD

poems by Sherod Santos

The Burning World
Sherod Santos

ISBN: 979-8-9863401-5-9

Boston — New York — San Francisco — Baghdad
San Juan — Kyiv — Istanbul — Santiago, Chile
Beijing — Paris — London — Cairo — Madrid
Milan — Melbourne — Jerusalem — Darfur

11 Chestnut St.
Medford, MA 02155

arrowsmithpress@gmail.com
www.arrowsmithpress.com

The forty-seventh Arrowsmith book
was typeset & designed by Ezra Fox
for Askold Melnyczuk & Alex Johnson
in Baskerville font

Cover art by Sherod Santos, *Untitled, IV*,
gouache and watercolor on photographic paper, 2022

TABLE OF CONTENTS

HAVING ALREADY INVENTED THE GREEKS

Nothing much left to talk about
beyond the iron law the hero
butchered on the battlefield pierced
through the tendons ankle-
to-heel no different now

>   *an outcrop of cloud a sense of place*
>   *of blood-spill spreading in parabolic loops*
>   *the warhorse drags the hero round*
>   *and thereby leaves the ill-starred*
>   *man-at-arms unsung*

will the story never stop
to read our minds to mark our place
in the margins and set aside
the wayward gods clairvoyants made
a metaphor for who we are?

I

THE ARDENT WEST

The metaled vanes
>of an eagle winged in heavy weather
cross the compound boundary walls
>>sun burning down in the massifs
creosote dumps in the plains burning down
>somewhere beyond the Republic's range
the shadow of a great bird falls.

THE EPIC

A war no mortal quarreled over
> ranked battalions bivouacked on the coast
> they left their country for
a hijacked bronze Sumerian nude by rights unsexed
> in the interest of Antiquity.

———

Favored by a pilot star
> bullhorned came the clarion call
> to raise the camps set torches out
in single file like runway lights
> and leave the rest to heaven help us god forbid
daybreak without warning comes...

———

...and calls to mind
> the parachute flare above the Golden Gate
that launched ten thousand goose-feathered arrows
> toward the dug-in men-of-war.

———

In the beginning, then, there was burned grass
      scorched stone
Myrmidons aping their shadows where
      no moon- or sunlight shone.

————

Think of the drone
      that filled the air above the armory
    of all that's left the stateless king
roped to a post at the beachhead
      his eyelids cut from his eyes
    his tears a violet iodine.

————

In voices lowered for the dead
      the tide through the kelp beds drawn
    the sound it makes an elegy
for Andromeda
      a drowsing lookout looks upon (far
    from his home in Appalachia)
to the sound of broadcast
      nightly prayers.

THE NOISE OF THE STARS

Having breached the concrete palisades
    the armored columns closed their ranks
  around a flagstaff at the Palace door
before the Great Bear intervened
    bisecting a floodlit quadrant of sky
  the closing Black Hawks sighted on.

LUNAR REDDENED

Blood-pigmented parapets instilled within us

    the aura of a ONE-AND-ONLY-

GOD.

    What could we do but recreate it in kind?

Oh, but we did don't you remember:

    the trussed-up ceremonial dead

the sound of shaken bottle-trees

    the overloaded tonnage scoop the earth like spoons?

————

Each armored convoy had in mind the land was theirs

to walk upon

    schoolgirls camouflaged as olive trees

phenol clouds shadowing the river

    a looted palace where once upon a time

a seabird's blue egg fashioned out of glass

    was served up daily in the citadel.

————

Laptops wired for all the languages foreign at first
       wired the barricades
wired the vest-packed shadows
       wired the wren on the radio
unheard over the drone.

———

Somewhere beyond the perimeter
       a three-legged dog sits out eternity yawning on the sands.

———

A day played back:

a man pulls a woman from the rubble and lays her by
       (children in the courtyard
playing like the man, one dressed up in window glass)
       the woman apparently with no legs
one brick stacked on another.

———

Asked what life was like for them
       (CNN WORLD NEWS)
young widows built a thorn fire

each tossed a peacock feather in.

———

Left open on the desktops
        textbooks on the Science of Anxiety
(year of publication: 2003):
        a problem / a theorem / a proof
a fractured chair embellished with
        bookmark flowers of drying blood.

———

There were animals in the suburbs large enough to eat
        barrel culverts cordoning off the housing blocks
the shadow-prints of refugees
        who walked the black approaches to the well.

———

Let alone still
        a cindered wind raked the sands (Sign of the Stranger
and Caul)
        let alone still the moon left on overnight so long
its filament waned
        let alone still those who died accounted for
the remnants of another unremarkable war.

IN SIREN TIMES

Paris, 1968

A scorched rain fell
        the capital alleyways overfilled
quartier cobbles launched a renaissance lifted a firebrand
to our age
        our fetish from
the mouth of the barrier bridges poured.

Bussed-in soldiers did not dwell upon barricade fires
        and sudden at our side
                the first smoke's reddish weight
blackened the monumental bronze.

Said and done *"a great principle of violence dictated our fashions"*
(Anabasis)
        and this was no time to tell us no
what passed for empire
        nomad law declared our common ground.

II

THE BURNING WORLD

satellites are spinning
— Sun Ra

1.

Firelight on water.
Equatorial calms.
A cumulous cloud
that loses itself
in the Atlantic deeps.

For a boy in love with war games, globes,
and aerial maps,
the world's as wide
as its armies on the eminence are,
and wider still
when late at night it's lit by a stylus
penlight beam.

So who's to blame if on such nights
he's carried away

on the tidal washings of a digital feed?
He takes a deep breath, and

like some new conscript
cleaning the breech
of an M-16,
he imagines himself in body armor
advancing atop an M1A1
Abrams through

Al-Qaim, Anah, Haditha, Hīt.

2.

And you?

I'll tell you what the wisest do
those lovers of absolute zero
at the bone, they pursue
their dreams through
the high-rise
of a glass
syringe.

So why not empty

your carry-on

and from

its twice-stitched lining draw

a spoonful of

the stardust you have

smuggled in?

Let mind's eye

see what eyes

have seen.

3.

"I've seen creosoted Hebron skies.

Afghan peaks that burn all night

like something wired. Beneath

a Kurdish sun, I've seen a woman

with an infant in a burlap bag.

And yet, despite the occasional suicide bomb…"

Yes?

"I'm bored."

Like an eco-
tourist as the tour winds down,
he can't help feel the last resort
was just another rock-heap bleached
by guano and mollusk shells.

Time stops.
Restarts.
Applause.

4.

Leaning against the wet zinc of a seaside bar,

"So where you off to now?"
"Home."
"Where's home?"
"Wherever it is, whenever I get there, no one takes me in."

The barkeep wipes the counter down
and shares his view.

5.

So,

come

HOLIDAY IN

THE OLD-WORLD CHARM

OF MAZATLÁN

' where torchbearers hauled up

heavenward on ropes

slip-knotted around their feet

upend a Mesoamerica

the Julian calendar slashed and burned.

Thorn forest tended like a putting green.

The wingtip of a parasail.

The gated habitat of polished stone.

"It reminds me of Palm Springs!"

And this we call: EXPERIENCE.

6.

Cut to:

The gangway.

"And now?"
"Now what?"
"What's next?"

"Whatever's listed on the manifest."

Atacama
Kyzyl-kum
Namib
Kalahari
Thar

The penlight spot blinks out.
The armies wait.
Horseflies cross the air in droves.

III

BY NOW A BLACK FLAG WAVED

Highlighted by magnesium flares

    the shoreline tided in ruin

the scansion of oar-strokes

    pilot whales tow heavenward.

CIMETIÈRE DES INNOCENTS

Ossuary catacombs

{*Empire de la Mort*}

bone-piles dim-lit storied with slogans

hemp rope cordage

a guiding hand abided by

to walk the silent visitors through.

ON THE BATTERY SIDE OF THE ISLAND

Sandbars where the lionhearted were purified
and set afloat. Barrel fires roasting nightingales.
Bottle glass in the Ditch of Thieves. The hum
of flies from a decommissioned satellite dish.
Another flag, another ruin, another marble god.
Another man's version of the Promised Land.

ROULETTE BIAS

Screened off by plate glass paravents
the migraine clatter coming up 0
before the full moon rose in windowed
livery and raked the collared spoils in.

FRAGMENTS FROM A VANISHED CITY

i.

Conjured from clay vessels

     in immortal robes
a Lord in all senses left where he fell
       beyond believing
the blood-sport vandals loosed upon the land.

ii.

Iron-gated palace rooms

     where cobras charmed their handlers
and women who would save themselves
       stained their teeth with pomegranate seed.

iii.

On the underground columbarium walls

     { hieroglyphs of filament mold }

iv.

In sand it's writ

      the battle was foreshortened by
the eiderdown of an emperor goose
           picked clean by the Sun God
feasting overhead.

v.

Hatched from a Sunburst Centuries Ago

      brazier-blackened squat on her heels
her eyes opalescent as the eggs of spiders
          Allah she said
her hand upholding a missing sphere.

vi.

Cuneiformed in the mineral dark

      the paling traces of a dead
Amorite language
         schoolboys with detectors
sweep for coins.

IV

THE SIBYL POEMS

Undressed in the shadow of the Appalachian hills, the scent of pine straw, cattle, heat. Twice-witnessed waist-deep in the green-water quarry, a red bandana covered her wet. The tall grass swayed, a pickup idled on the trestle bridge. Even climbing vines made a myth of her.

ILIUM

Viaduct blue with rainwater, blue the streetlight

shadowing the café, blue the clarion

carafe of ash, black tobacco's bluish haze.

From the dead-end alleyway, tallow of sex

and garbage, everything blue and ripening.

In the shadow dancer's almond eyes an insect

craving the insect gods for their brief lives abided by.

And who are we to live beyond her ecstasy

if not to carry on, if not in Heaven here,

on this our more or less common ground?

OVERLOOKED BY THE HIGH-STRUNG MOON

Her almond eyes mascaraed with a thin
tin liner dowel from a Bedouin mint-colored
kohl bag tethered to a cord around her neck.
He said once to her spidery with want
he saw in the glow of an electric coil the vein
in her neck contract. Her feathered flesh
adored her, her bangled bracelets sounding
through a drainpipe overhead, and when
it tasted like blood to her, her sugared voice
bore witness to a side of her that likes
the taste her bite mark left him tender from.
It was in her nature, after all, pleasure
and pain being what they are to the abstract
goddess she'd changed back into overnight.

DELIRIUM

Fan blades rounding on the backs of flies,
sun like a vacuum sack of blood, a sliding scale
on the clouding barrel of a locked syringe.

GLASS HOUSE

No one thinks to come back after you die,
and yet you did. A bolt-hole basement
near the shipping yard, a rabbit cage mattress
on the floor, a pin-pricked pomegranate seed,
a molten spoon, the chimneyed foil,
the nodding over from time to time, the nodding out

half a life ago your hair's on fire

*

Eyes closed against the flame,
you heard above you a hummingbird's hum,
the hummingbird high in the head

above you in your bed-sick bed

*

Your face gone rose a cross perhaps
or some other ornament around your neck,

your gaze turned inward and looked upon

a fever bird cross the clockless wall

*

I checked you into an anteroom
checked you life-like breathing in

Homeless as a runaway, you paced
the talcumed 12 ft. floor from end to end
and were not moved to speak

or say

you couldn't see why
you'd come back only long enough
(and then so long ago)
to leave the impression elegies leave

a brother a sister a parent a child

WHERE ONCE A TREE WITH GREEN BUDS

Rolled molten metal roofs. Remnants of cinder
the conflagration was. Trees but not the shadows
of trees. Hardscrabble, shell-money, knucklebone
foraged from the burn

      cowbirds circling the kneeling pilgrims.

IN HER LAST DREAM

Carried away on bare feet to the greenhouse
  packed with catalogue vines.
In those days hummingbirds too, and the coal
  smoke omen of a passenger train.

NOTES

"In Siren Times"   Student riots, Paris, 1968

"The Burning World"   Baudelaire's *Le Voyage*
                              is invoked in a number
                              of passages.

"Roulette Bias"   Tesuque Pueblo Casino,
                              New Mexico, 2018

"Cimetière des Innocents" The oldest cemetery in Paris.
                              In the Middle ages, it was the
                              site of mass graves, and when
                              space eventually ran out, the
                              bones were exhumed and
                              stacked in charnel houses
                              and catacombs that ran
                              beneath the city.

ACKNOWLEDGMENTS

This book is dedicated to Lynne McMahon.

I would like to thank the editor and publisher of *Arrowsmith*, Askold Melnyczuk, novelist, essayist, poet, translator, and tireless activist on behalf of the Ukrainian people. In his life and work, the intersection of literature and politics is not an abstract idea but an everyday reality. I would also like to thank Rosanna Warren, an education unto herself, one I've learned a great deal from over the years.

Grateful acknowledgment is made to Senior Editor Ezra Fox, whose insights and design skills have been a great help in shaping this book; and to the editors of the following journals: *Boston Review, Broad Street, Innisfree Poetry Journal, Kenyon Review, Literary Imagination (Oxford University Press), New American Writing, Paris Review, Poem-a-Day (Academy of American Poets), Raritan, Yale Review, Visible Binary.*

Poet, playwright and translator, Sherod Santos is the author of seven books of poetry, most recently *Square Inch Hours*. A National Book Award, *New Yorker* Book Award and National Book Critics Award Finalist, in 1999 he received an Award for Literary Excellence from the American Academy of Arts and Letters. He has taught at several universities in the United States and was Poet-in-Residence at the former Poets' House in Belfast, Northern Ireland. He currently lives in Santa Fe, where he works with a hunger relief program serving nine counties in Northern New Mexico.

Books by

ARROWSMITH
PRESS

Girls by Oksana Zabuzhko

Bula Matari/Smasher of Rocks by Tom Sleigh

This Carrying Life by Maureen McLane

Cries of Animals Dying by Lawrence Ferlinghetti

Animals in Wartime by Matiop Wal

Divided Mind by George Scialabba

The Jinn by Amira El-Zein

Bergstein
edited by Askold Melnyczuk

Arrow Breaking Apart by Jason Shinder

Beyond Alchemy by Daniel Berrigan

Conscience, Consequence: Reflections on Father Daniel Berrigan
edited by Askold Melnyczuk

Ric's Progress by Donald Hall

Return To The Sea by Etnairis Rivera

The Kingdom of His Will by Catherine Parnell

Eight Notes from the Blue Angel by Marjana Savka

Fifty-Two by Melissa Green

Music In—And On—The Air by Lloyd Schwartz

Magpiety by Melissa Green

Reality Hunger by William Pierce

Soundings: On The Poetry of Melissa Green
edited by Sumita Chakraborty

The Corny Toys by Thomas Sayers Ellis

Black Ops by Martin Edmunds

Museum of Silence by Romeo Oriogun

City of Water by Mitch Manning

Passeggiate by Judith Baumel

Persephone Blues by Oksana Lutsyshyna

The Uncollected Delmore Schwartz
edited by Ben Mazer

The Light Outside by George Kovach

The Blood of San Gennaro by Scott Harney
edited by Megan Marshall

No Sign by Peter Balakian

Firebird by Kythe Heller

cont...

ARROWSMITH is named after the late William Arrowsmith, a renowned classics scholar, literary and film critic. General editor of thirty-three volumes of *The Greek Tragedy in New Translations*, he was also a brilliant translator of Eugenio Montale, Cesare Pavese, and others. Arrowsmith, who taught for years in Boston University's University Professors Program, championed not only the classics and the finest in contemporary literature, he was also passionate about the importance of recognizing the translator's role in bringing the original work to life in a new language.

Like the arrowsmith who turns his arrows straight and true,
a wise person makes his character straight and true.

— Buddha

www.ingramcontent.com/pod-product-compliance
Lightning Source LLC
Chambersburg PA
CBHW030519130626
46549CB00007B/3059